Dancing with Transcendence in Nature's Embrace

Britteny Corrin Godar

Presentation by *BookLeaf Publishing*

Web: www.bookleafpub.com

E-mail: info@bookleafpub.com

ISBN: 9789358319446

First edition 2024

I dedicate this book to

*the sweetest, sassiest, and naughtiest joy of
my life,*

my beloved doggie soul mate for eternity,

Kamala.

ACKNOWLEDGEMENT

I would like to thank my soul dog, Kamala, for fundamentally changing the soul that I am.

I would also like to thank her doggie death doula and vets who allowed her to have a fulfilled and dignified life and a peaceful passing.

I thank her photographer that helped me capture beautiful moments with Kamala that I can see to evoke my memories.

PREFACE

Dancing with Transcendence in Nature's Embrace explores metamorphosis, the cyclical nature of the universe, the blossoms and the decay, and, ultimately, spins you into nature's dances.

It takes you through deep canyons, grandiose mountains, moon cycles, turbulent oceans, wandering rivers, whirling wind, and the inevitable sunrise and sunset. It is an immersion in wisdom, absurdity, transitions, transcendence, and the enduring and scattered energy of the soul. It brings you to embrace all the high leaps, low curtsies, and twirls in your own life's dance.

It is a tale of love, loss, and love again ignited by the tail of a precious dog, of a life force.

Dancing with Grief

Grief is a cyclical, unexpected villain.

All you can learn is to dance with
disappointment,
twirling in the face of shattered expectations.

Embrace revelations living in loss
to empower your wisdom
without dismantling your soul.

Double Sided Waltz

2

Two sides of the same coin.
The dark and light.
The yin and yang.

Love's levitation
is of equal expanse
to grief's deep cuts.

The Body's Curtsy

I promised you
when your little body was places in my hands,
I would offer you the best life possible,
which implied the best death possible,
peacefully in my arms,
when a life worth living was no longer an
option.

You said to me, my body was done.
Period.

I lay here with you on the floor.

I hate that the sun is rising
because I know it will be your last.

I am relieved the sun is rising
because you didn't have a traumatic death in the
night
and struggles are coming to pass.

I cannot control
the sun rising,
nor the sun setting.

Bodies come and go,
like the sun rises and sets
but love is eternal.

Nature's Ballet

Dawn breaks the stage.

Light dancing on the canyon.
Squirrels jumping joyfully.
Leaves twirling around.
Glittering snow thrown about.

Glows curtsy over the mountain tops.
Suns wave to the crowd.
Moons and darkness dim the theater.

Thank you for dancing with me.

Dancing with Tantalizing Tarantulas

I found something that I believed was nothing.

As I lay on the Vortex,
the Sky opened in it's circle.

Everything is in circles and cycles.

Piecing pain on my right forehead,
was it a pain or release?
A painful release
of self-made Guilt.

I held my Guilt tightly and gently,
as I would hold her,
I made Guilt fill my vast void,
even though It sought to diminish
the existence of present Love.

I visualized the vibrant hot air balloon
lifting enormously heavy Guilt from my mind
and floating into the glaring red and orange
sculpted rocks
in the blazing hot sunset
until I could no longer see it

among the luminescent Sky hues.

Such a relief to cut the ties
and release my firm agreement
to everlasting Guilt.

I let Guilt go into the ether,
walked with her playful ghost
as she wagged and wandered
on the dust trail
blanketed by Love.

She was not restrained,
only Instinctual,
and Free.

But my agreement with Guilt
was attempting to sabotage me as I
moved further from the Vortex.

The Judge and Watcher in my mind were a war.
Like being stuck in war,
I couldn't find a path out.

I saw a gigantic flower
with a white center
and black petals.

It grew,

expanding tremendously
in the dusk light.

It's petals emerging,
It did a ballet number of
assembles and piles.

The flower began spinning and sprinting,
It was a Tarantula!

With Laughter and Splendor,
I was delighted to be surprised
right into the present moment
with Love
and was grateful to be saved by
dancing with a tantalizing tarantula.

I Saw You There

Walking through the dunes this morning,
I saw the moon and knew it was you
transforming.

The yellow flower the ones like we used to wear
in our hair,
was your bright wild-eyed stare.

I can't just keep holding onto your old memories
when I know you are anew,
even the Driftwood has wandered out into the
vast blue.

Our footsteps and pawprints constantly engulfed
by the ocean
with the waxing and waning tides.
The ocean has come to take us together on a
rejuvenating ride.

Planting my Mind in Light

While I cared for my "old" plants,
my sentient and sentimental ones,
I planted new herbs that I knew would die
Because I was going to eat them,
But I planted them anyways…
Like I do the thoughts in my head,
As my mind ponders absurdities and
impermenacies.

At this moment, in the window,
I adjust my old plants to let the new ones in.
Arranging them with intention,
They can co-exist
Without the new ones being stifled
Or the old ones being forgotten.

Planting in the finest place,
Let me be right here,
Right now,
In the glowing sunshine in the window.

Sisyphus, how long must I Dance?

With each aging day,
I come to know and become my good friend,
Sisyphus.

I ask my friend Sisyphus, how long must I
dance?

Finding purpose in the mundane.
Continuing my own life and creating death,
only to prolong my suffering.

When is enough, enough?
When purposes cease to exist.

My attempts towards mindfulness of everyday
survival tasks while dying
are always ridiculous.

The absurdity is acknowledged by self,
but primal instincts protest and continue on their
march.

Here I surrender to the primal instincts and
mundane,

and continue dance.
Halleluiah Sisyphus.

Speck in a Theater

Drove through the Rockies-
It was confirmed,
I am a Speck.

As a Speck,
I understand purity,
As the rain and mountains collide.

As a Speck,
I understood uncertainty,
As a boulder innocently crashes down.

As a Speck,
I understand personality,
As the light illuminates the details of earth's
surface.

As a Speck,
I understand my spirit,
And that all Things have a spirit.

Resignation of Self Actualization

I see you grow and move.
From the static position in the chair to the vigor
of walking in the garden.
Many hours, motivating words and your hard
work.
Coming from a place of nearing the end to the
enjoyment of life.
Laughing with you.
Talking about the trains and the paintings.
Seeing the smile while we make movement.
Listening and really listening to your stories.
Intertwining your stories with mine.
Going along with your story that I am an old
friend even though we have only known each
other a few months.
And all the time and happiness is stolen by an
invisible terrorist, a killer, a torturer of life that
no one saw coming or cared to prepare for it's
coming.

The thoughts of all the effort thrown into the
rubbish.
These thoughts can only be met by the opposite
in order to carry on.

The time spent was the only personal time spent
for those that could never see their families,
maybe never again.
The time spent was to make a joyful experience
in that moment.
The effort exerted may have been the only
defense against the terrorist even though the war
was lost.

Why to continue?
The answer is in the negative.
Why not to continue?
Because I am positive in my inability to take
action not to continue.
Why even look that direction.

Before the terrorist arrived, I knew I had to give
my glory away.
Society did not honor my type of warrior and
burned my warrior tribe to the ground when the
terrorist came. They did not support the war.
They wanted the warriors to die in the was like
throwing sticks in a flame with no regard to the
campfire structure. No light would be made,
only unnecessary sacrifices.

Before the bare exposures, before needless
insults, before the exhaustion, before the

suffocation, you had taken the opportunity to oppress your essential warriors. How are we even standing after years of war waged on us while out only intentions are to save those in the world.

The realization is like the reverse metamorphosis without the organism's control.

I give it away.
I give it away as I give away my ambitions, any belief in human decency, any trajectory towards true health and any true sense of actualization.

My Resignation of Self Actualization.

I burn my passport in resistance of expeditions.
I sell my wetsuit and dreams of continued big blue exploration.
My camera flies out the window to crash my captures of unseen moments and memories.
My dresses are bleached to make cloths to wipe the wretched water on this destroyed face.
The jewelry will be buried with the memories of the artists meetings.
My shoes rot with the lack of dance, dinners and galloping.
The fancy hats collect dust and to dust they shall return.

The artwork only serves as a slap to the jaw that
joyous life is in the past and will never be
spoken of in the future.

The joy of attaining the thing, the experience,
the prestige is only to be muffled and diluted by
the great sorrow of giving the thing and the
symbolism of the thing away with your soul.

Please accept this as my Resignation of Self
Actualization.

The Why

There is no why.

Subsequently, Death is a nominal treaty with the Taos.

Logically, the path of least resistance to death is evolutionary.

I will take the energy

Deplete it

To the mountain

And disperse it

With the opium

In the forbidden land

Because curiosity is natural

And so is Death.

The Pronghorn

I was thinking nothing at all.
I felt a void,
Talked of a void,
Spoke your name.

Your song came,
You showed me beauty,
As I was defining beauty,
Through twist and turn in the Wyoming
wilderness,
A pronghorn,
You showed me,
And your song,
The Highway men,
On a beautiful highway,
Through the medicine bow forest.

You were in my arms,
Head out the window, hair in the wind,
I released your hair into the wind,
You showed me your hair,
To let me know you were there,
And everywhere,
And in The pronghorn,
The ones I thought of as beauty,

To show me beauty.

To teach me perpetual flow,
However you want to call it-
Tao, flow, dispersed reincarnations,
Or to call it nothing at all.

With you Everywhere

My fur has turned to winter snow,
My nose to pink roses and red poppies.

My ears to the yellow flowers and the freckles
on my legs to spots of the sparkling sun.

My eyes to the full moon,
My hair to the sand dunes.

You feel me when you see a
Dogs ears flying in the to the autumn breeze,
Wet paw prints in park,
The dog beside you begging for food
 And defluffing the toys,
The odd noises at night are my dream sounds,
The sniffing, naught dog embodies me.

I am young and old, dead and alive and all are
wise.
I am flying high as your spirit guide bringing
you closer to who you are.
You looked out for me, we looked after each
other, and now I'm watching over you. One day
I will bring you with me.

Transversing Canyons

You led me through the slotted canyon
to watch the shimmering light and mysterious
shadows
make whispy illusions whilst
playing throughout the day, the night, and across
time.

You showed me that the reliable and stubborn
stone
could be cut by the shape-shifting water and ice.

The stone's resilient essence
could become waves of sand
when giving in to
the way of water.

The ability of the stone to feel
and water to move
let them know they share the same soul
while on this expedition through
the desert of impermanence.

Their dance is one of extraordinary beauty
for other spirits to see.

Yet, there would be no deep connection
to lay witness to if they had not collided
and transversed into the canyon.

Of Anti-Resilency and Movement

Be Resilient, they say.
But I do not wish to be Resilient.

Resilient is a rough, hard stone.
It is stuck, unmoved,
until it is pushed or thrown.

Resilient seems void of Growth,
but withers away slowly,
usually when it meets my Friends,
Water & Wind.

I want to embrace Water,
move around stones,
be fluid,
flexible,
follow my impermanence
and return to the Stream,
to Rain in the Clouds,
to Snow,
to Ice,
to Water.

Wisdom says to be Water's Reflection.

I want to entwine with Wind.
Be and feel a presence in the absence of seeing.
Be a cooling force when becoming too hot.
Pushing us in the direction we can go.
Making the Trees & Ocean Dance.

Wisdom lets us Play in the Wind.

You were the Whirling Wild Wind

You were as Wild as the Wind.

Whispy fur,
Whispering in your dreams,
Whirling and dancing for tricks,
Whining for treats,
Whistling to call you,
Whiskering,
Whipping your tail.
Wallowing in the grass,
Wickedly hunting squirrels,
Wandering through the woods
Welcoming strangers,
Wishing for more treats,
Willowing,
Woofing.

We were as Wild as the Whirling Wind.

Death of Young Flowering Dancers

Change is instinctive.

We honor the flows of life,
of Birth & Death,
Coming together & splitting apart.

Feeling the beauty in both
the flourishing, bright, young flower,
and the fading, drying, browning petals,
we find
Balance & Acceptance.

The Black Veil Costume

I never knew why women wore the Black Veil.

I had never before felt the grief that required the donning of a Black Veil until now.

Now, I understand and will never doff this Black Veil.

Now, I can only view the work with the darkness of the Black Veil.

Now, the Sun and everything it touches will never be allowed to illuminate so brightly and shimmer.

Now, the Black Veil is a permanent fixture on my head,
confining my mind,
reminding my soul.

But, it is okay because it reminds me of lovely You.

Flows of Letting Go

We took the flowers to the creek we used to
walk upon.

With each flower I threw in the water, I let go,
or at least tried to let go of some
fleeting thought of emotion,
a non-factual, feeling of an impulse
imprinted on my brain.

Letting go of Guilt & Anxiety,
that I would never, ever be a good dog or child
Mom.

Letting go of thinking something was wrong
if energy transitioned to something else,
which I will call life and death.

Letting go of the should-haves,
when very little would of changed
by a different action or inaction.

I watched as the flowers flew down the creek
where we used to walk, sniff, and gawk.

Some floated easily over the rapids in the high
and violent Creek
and drifted on beautifully with hesitations,
but others were Stuck.

Some took the long way around the stones in
their path.

Others that were previously floating became
Stuck,
much later,
further down-stream.

The Flows and Patience of Letting Go.

Better to Dance with you than Sit

I can walk through the park quickly,
but I would rather walk slowly,
watching You sniff every nook and cranny,
the dirt and the trees,
and try to eat everything.

I can go out with no regard for time,
but I would happily rush back if
I could see your excited, fluffy face.

I can stay in all Winter,
but I would happily bundle up
to watch You play in the Snow.

I have less bills,
but I would happily give all my money and
material things
to just hold You and make You Happy.

You are worth everything,
and I would trade it all to have you physically
back.

My Love's Next Act

The mountains with the sun and clouds put on a
new show every sunset.

The plains with the grass and bison paint with
wind and light a new picture each moment.

The dunes with the birds, oceans and shells
perform a transformative dance every new day.

Why would I ever expect you to be still and
stagnant.

You are still living,
just in a new way.

www.ingramcontent.com/pod-product-compliance
Lightning Source LLC
LaVergne TN
LVHW051241200726
843510LV00011B/1640